Contents

Introduction

Pompoms are really easy to make, and are a great way to use up all your yarn oddments. But what can you do with a pile of pompoms once you have made them? This book should provide you with plenty of ideas.

Every project is accompanied by clear instructions, which will help you to achieve perfect results. Start by following them to the letter, then use them to inspire your own creativity. Have fun!

Cherries

Make your keys stand out from the crowd with this fun and simple make. It can also be used to cheer up the zip-pull of a cardigan or anorak.

Materials

Small pompom maker
Oddment of deep red 3- or 4-ply yarn
Oddment of brown chunky yarn
Scrap of green felt
All-purpose adhesive
Sharp scissors
Darning needle
Plain keyring

Tip
Make a brooch by sewing a small safety pin to the back of the leaves.

Method

1 Make two pompoms and trim down until they are smooth, spherical and the size required, cutting off the ends of the yarn used to tie them.

2 Cut two lengths of brown yarn and tie a double knot in the end of each.

3 Thread a length of brown yarn on to the needle and run it carefully through the centre of one of the cherries. The yarn knot will be buried in the pile of the pompom. Repeat with the second cherry.

4 Cut two pieces of green felt, each 1¼ x ⅝in (3 x 1.5cm). Trim the ends of each carefully to make leaf shapes.

5 Knot the ends of the brown yarn together and sew or glue the leaves together in front of the knot.

6 Loop the yarn through the keyring to attach the cherries.

Chick

This chirpy little creature is an ideal project when you need to amuse children on a rainy afternoon. Why not create a whole clutch of chicks, varying each slightly to give them individual personalities?

Materials

Very small and small
    pompom makers
Yellow 4-ply yarn
Small piece of red EVA
    sheet or felt
All-purpose adhesive
Two 5–6mm black beads
Pointed tweezers
Sharp scissors
Darning needle
Clothes pegs
Pencil

Method

1 Make one very small and one small pompom and trim to shape, leaving the ends of yarn used to tie the pompoms long.

2 Tie the two pompoms together very firmly. Thread a needle with the ends of yarn, one at a time, and run them back and forth through the pompoms for extra strength.

3 Trim the pompoms carefully into a chick shape, flattening the bottom of the larger pompom a little so that it will sit upright.

4 Cut two small triangles from EVA sheet or felt, then trim each one carefully into a foot shape. If you want to use felt for the feet, glue two identical triangles together before shaping for extra strength.

5 Cover the back of the foot shapes with a layer of adhesive and position under the larger pompom. Leave to dry.

6 Cut two rectangles of EVA sheet or felt approx. 1¼ x ⅜in (3 x 1cm). Shape one side of each into a curve to form wings.

7 Using the blade of the scissors, part the yarn near the top of the larger pompom. Squeeze adhesive along the channel and push one wing shape firmly in, with the straight side forward. Pinch the yarn over the wing to cover the join. Repeat with the other wing. Allow the adhesive to dry, holding the wings in place with pegs if necessary.

Tip
Feathers in a matching shade also make effective wings.

8 Using the point of a pencil, part the yarn of the smaller pompom and squeeze a blob of adhesive into the indentation created. Using tweezers, place a small black bead on the blob of adhesive. Repeat for the other eye.

9 Cut two tiny triangles from EVA sheet or felt and join them at the base using adhesive. Part the yarn of the smaller pompom beneath the eyes, squeeze in a small blob of adhesive and push the beak firmly in. Pinch the yarn over the join and allow to dry.

10 Part the two triangles of the beak using the point of the scissors.

Bunny

Another really easy make, this little bunny has arms made from a chenille stick wrapped in yarn and is carrying a pretty flower.

Materials

Very small, small and medium
   pompom makers
4-ply or DK yarn
Oddment of pink yarn
Scraps of pink, red and green felt
2 x 5–6mm black beads
One small pink bead
A chenille stick
All-purpose adhesive
Sharp scissors and pointed tweezers
Clothes peg or paper clip
Pencil

Method

1 Make one small pompom and one medium pompom, leaving the ends used to tie them long. Tie the pompoms together firmly, then thread each free end on a large darning needle and run back and forth through both pompoms for additional security.

2 Trim the pompoms to shape, flattening the bottom of the larger pompom slightly so the bunny will stand up.

3 Cut two rectangles of pink felt, each about ⅜ x ⅝in (1.5 x 1cm). Trim one end of each into a point to shape the ears.

4 Squeeze a small blob of adhesive onto the flat end of each ear shape and fold the sides to the middle. Use a peg or paper clip to hold the ear together as the adhesive dries.

5 Part the yarn at the top of the smaller pompom using the blade of the scissors and squeeze adhesive into the channel made. Insert the ears firmly into the channel, pinching the yarn over them to hide the join.

6 Using the point of a pencil, part the yarn at the points where you want to place the eyes. Squeeze a small blob of adhesive into each and carefully insert the black beads using pointed tweezers.

7 Using a pencil, part the yarn where you want to place the nose and squeeze in a small blob of adhesive. Position the pink bead using the tweezers.

8 Using the pink yarn, make a very small pompom. Sew or attach with adhesive to the back of the bunny.

9 Fold the chenille stick sides to the middle and twist to form the arms. Wind grey yarn evenly round the chenille stick, attaching the ends of the yarn firmly with adhesive.

Tip

If you like, you can make a whole bunch of flowers for the bunny to hold.

10 Part the yarn at the back of the bunny's neck using the blade of the scissors and squeeze adhesive along the channel formed. Lay the centre of the length of wrapped chenille stick along the channel and pinch the yarn over it. Allow to dry, holding in place with pegs if necessary.

11 Cut a flower shape from the red felt and a leaf and stem from the green felt. Sew the flower to the stem using contrasting yarn.

12 Attach the flower to one of the bunny's arms and bend the arms into shape.

Garland

This bright garland is an effective alternative to bunting. The pompoms are simply threaded on fine organza ribbon, so it is really easy to make.

Materials

Pompom maker
Yarn
Sharp scissors
Reel of organza ribbon
Darning needle

Method

1 Decide how long you want your garland to be and how far apart you plan to place each pompom. In the example shown, the pompoms are about 3½in (9cm) apart.

2 Make the required number of pompoms and lay them out in a pleasing configuration. It is best to aim for an uneven number of pompoms, so that when threading you can work back in either direction from a central pompom.

3 Cut the ribbon to length, allowing extra for tying the hanging loops on the end. Remember that garlands fall in a gentle loop or loops, so do not cut the ribbon too short.

4 Thread one end of the ribbon on the darning needle. Part the centre pompom to find the hole in the centre of where the ends were tied. Carefully insert the needle and pull the ribbon gently through. Hold the pompom firmly as you work and take care not to dislodge any of the wool strands.

5 Slide the pompom carefully to the exact centre of the ribbon. Add the adjacent pompom in the same way, sliding it into position at the required distance. Continue until one side of the garland has been threaded.

6 Thread the other end of the ribbon on the needle, then complete the second half of the garland.

7 Check the spacing between the pompoms, then double over the ends of the ribbon and tie a hanging loop in each. Trim the ends of the ribbon fairly close to the knot.

8 Hang both loops of the garland from a suitable hook – I used a picture hook – and check whether any of the pompoms need a final trim.

Tip

Be as creative as you like with your pompoms, varying the sizes, shades used and the distance between each.

Mouse

This little mouse is the perfect size for a mischievous child to keep in a pocket – grannies beware! It also makes a fun plaything for a favourite cat.

Materials

Very small and small pompom makers
Small ball of grey fluffy 4-ply or DK yarn
Oddment of brown chunky yarn
Scrap of pink felt
2 x 5–6mm black beads
All-purpose adhesive
Small crochet hook
Sharp scissors and pointed tweezers
Short length of fishing line (optional)
Clothes pegs
Pencil

Method

1 Make one small pompom and one very small pompom, leaving the ends used to tie them long. Tie them together firmly, then thread each free end on a large darning needle and run back and forth through both pompoms for additional security.

2 Trim the mouse to shape, giving it a pointed nose and slimming down the body.

3 Cut two rectangles of pink felt, each about ⅜ x ⅝in (1.5 x 1cm). Trim one end of each to make a rounded ear shape.

4 Using the blade of the scissors part the yarn at the back of the smaller pompom and squeeze adhesive into the channel made.

5 Insert the ears firmly into the channel, pinching the yarn over them to hide the join. Allow the adhesive to dry, holding the ears in place with pegs if necessary.

6 Using the point of a pencil, part the yarn at the points where you want to place the eyes. Squeeze adhesive into each indentation.

7 Using pointed tweezers, carefully position the beads on the blobs of adhesive.

8 Using the yarn and small crochet hook, make a 4in (20cm) length of chain (see page 48) to form a tail. Fasten off, leaving a long end.

9 Thread the long yarn end on a large sharp needle and attach the tail firmly by sewing into the pompom several times. Sew in the other end of yarn.

10 Cut three or four short lengths of fishing line to form whiskers. Make a channel at the tip of the nose and squeeze in adhesive, then lay the whiskers across. Pinch the yarn over the whiskers until the adhesive dries.

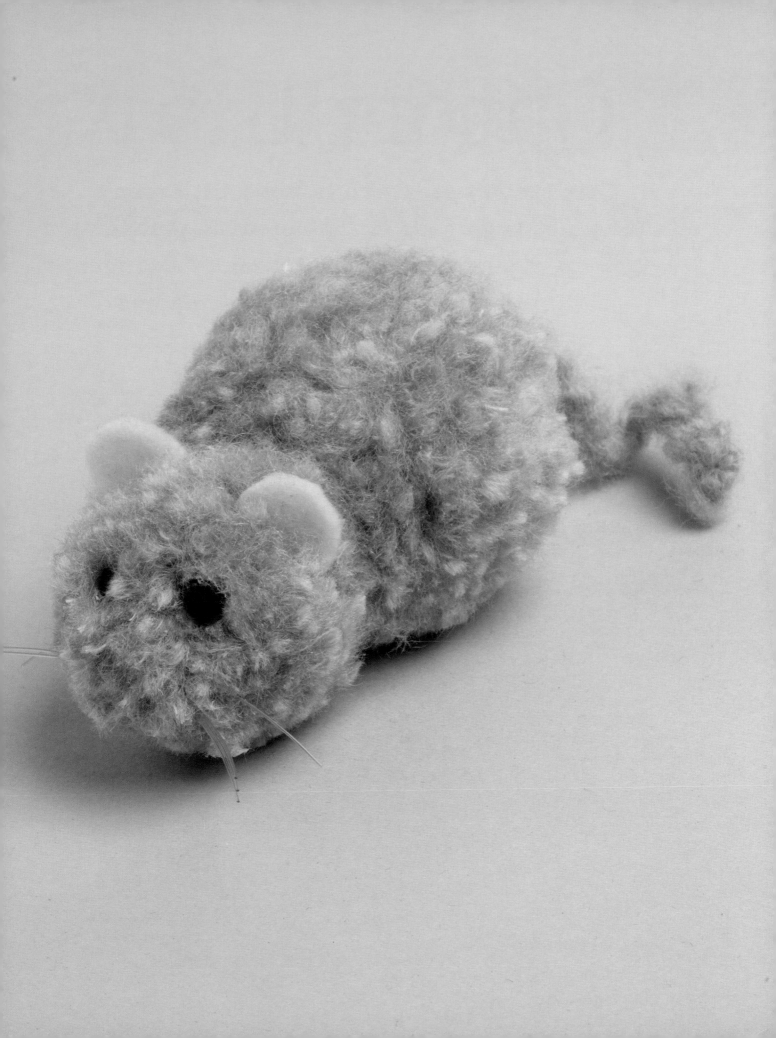

Caterpillar

This crawly creature is not a bit creepy. Why not try using multi-coloured pompoms for an eye-catching look, or make a longer caterpillar by adding extra pompoms?

Materials

Small, medium and
   large pompom makers
50g ball of 4-ply yarn
Purple chenille stick
Two medium self-adhesive
   googly eyes
Sharp scissors
Darning needle
Round-nose pliers
Knitting needle or chopstick

Method

1   Make four small pompoms, three medium pompoms and one large pompom, leaving long yarn ends after tying them.

2   Trim the pompoms carefully, making sure that each has a good round shape.

3   Tie two small pompoms together securely. Thread the yarn ends on a large needle and run through the opposite side of the second pompom, ready to tie to the third pompom.

4   Tie the second and third pompoms together securely. Thread the yarn ends on a large needle and run through to the opposite side of the third pompom.

5   Continue in this way until all the pompoms are joined together. Sew the final yarn ends individually through the large pompom several times for extra security.

6   Fold the purple chenille stick ends to the middle and twist to secure.

7   Holding the join at the centre, insert a knitting needle or chopstick in the loop at one end. Wind round to form a twist. Repeat with the other end, winding it in the opposite direction.

8   Place the twisted stick between the head pompom and the next, and twist round the neck to form antennae.

9   Position the googly eyes and press firmly into place.

Tip

Make a stretchy caterpillar by threading the pompoms on round cord elastic instead of tying them together.

Spider

The biggest, fluffiest spider you will ever see is also the friendliest, so even determined arachnophobes may decide he's a new friend.

Materials

Large and medium
  pompom makers
50g black 4-ply or DK yarn
9 thick, black chenille
  craft sticks
Pair of 7mm self-adhesive
  googly eyes
All-purpose adhesive
Large darning needle
Sharp scissors
Small pair of pliers
Knitting needle or pencil

Tip

For a small spider, use medium and small pompoms. Make each double leg with a single folded and twisted chenille stick.

Method

1 Make one large pompom and one medium pompom. Trim, leaving the threads used to tie them off long for joining the pompoms together.

2 Knot the pompoms together firmly, then thread the ends on to a darning needle, one at a time, and sew them back and forth through the spider's body for extra security.

3 Twist two chenille sticks together, then turn the ends under using the pliers to shape them. Repeat to make four double 'legs'.

4 Lay the legs flat, parallel to each other. Weave the last chenille stick in and out through the legs to secure them and make a flat base for attaching to the spider.

5 Part the pile of the large pompom on the underside of the spider's body and spread with adhesive. Attach the raft of legs, pushing it firmly into the pile of the pompom. Hold in place with elastic bands until the adhesive dries.

6 Using the end of a knitting needle or pencil, make two slight indentations in the yarn at the points where you want to place the eyes.

7 Press the eyes carefully into position.

Sheep

Silly sheep are always popular, and this plump beauty has real appeal. You could experiment with different types of yarn, varying the shades used for the legs and face.

Materials

Small and large pompom makers
Variegated textured wool DK
    or Aran-weight yarn
Two thick chenille sticks
Oddment of black yarn
Scrap of black felt
2 self-adhesive googly eyes
All-purpose adhesive
Sharp scissors
Round-nose pliers
Small crochet hook
Darning needle
Knitting needle or chopstick
Clothes pegs or paper clips

Method

1   Make one large and one small pompom. Leave the ends of yarn used for tying them long, but do not trim the pompoms.

2   Knot the pompoms together firmly. Thread the ends of yarn on a darning needle, one at a time, and sew them back and forth through both pompoms for extra security.

3   Cut two squares of black felt, each with sides about 2½in (6cm) long. Coat one square with adhesive and join it to the other square, securing with pegs or paper clips if necessary. Leave to dry.

4   Fold each chenille stick end to the middle and secure by twisting together. Holding the twist at the centre, place a knitting needle or chopstick in the loop at the end and twist. Repeat with the other end, twisting in the opposite direction.

5   Wrap the sticks with yarn, sewing the ends of yarn over the foot loops for a tidy finish. Bend both sets of legs into a 'U' shape.

6   Using the blade of the scissors, part the yarn towards the front of the larger pompom and squeeze adhesive into the channel formed.

7   Lay the top of the 'U' into the channel and pinch the yarn over it to secure. Repeat with the other set of legs and set aside for the adhesive to dry. If necessary, hold the legs in place using pegs.

8 Trace and cut out the face template below and lay it on the square of felt. Now carefully cut out the face shape.

9 Coat the back of the face with adhesive and press into position on the small pompom. It does not matter if it's at a slight angle, as this just seems to give the sheep its personality.

10 Using the tweezers, place the googly eyes fairly close together and roughly in line with the bottom of the ears. Apply pressure to make sure they are firmly attached.

11 Make a short crocheted chain (see page 48) or plait for the tail with the oddment of black yarn. Coat one end with adhesive and push into the sheep's rear using the tweezers. Pinch the yarn strands from the pompom over the join and leave to dry.

12 Bend the legs into shape and set the sheep on its feet. Carefully trim the neck around the face shape if necessary.

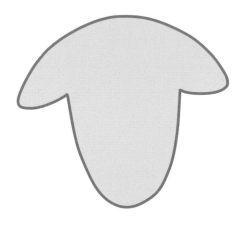

Tip

For a smaller sheep, use very small and medium pompom makers and scale down the template slightly.

Lamb

Here's a cute little lamb to accompany your silly sheep. Why not make a whole flock, giving each one a different body shape and facial features so they each have their own personality?

Materials

Small and medium pompom makers
Cream wool DK or Aran-weight yarn
2 x thick chenille sticks
Scraps of pink and cream felt
2 x 5–6mm black beads
All-purpose adhesive
Sharp scissors
Pointed tweezers
Darning needle
Small amount of cream wool
  roving (optional)
Knitting needle or chopstick
Clothes pegs

Method

1 Make one small pompom and one medium pompom, leaving the ends used to tie them long. Trim both pompoms into oval shapes. Do not throw away the trimmings as you will need them later.

2 Fold each chenille stick end to the middle and secure by twisting together. Holding the twist at the centre, place a knitting needle or chopstick in the loop at the end and twist. Repeat with the other end, twisting in the opposite direction.

3 Wrap each stick with yarn, sewing the ends over the foot loops for a tidy finish. Bend both sets of legs into a 'U' shape.

4 Tease out a length of wool roving and wrap each leg, joining in more roving as necessary and securing the ends with a tiny amount of adhesive. (This step may be omitted.)

5 Using the blade of the scissors, part the yarn towards the front of the larger pompom and squeeze adhesive into the channel formed.

6 Lay the top of the 'U' into the channel and pinch the yarn over it to secure the legs. Repeat with the other set of legs and set aside for the adhesive to dry. If necessary, hold the legs in place using pegs.

7 Adjust the legs until the lamb's body stands firmly. Place the head on the body and, when you are happy with the position, secure temporarily with adhesive.

8 Thread each long end of yarn on a large darning needle, one at a time, and use to secure the head firmly by running it back and forth through both pompoms. Trim the head to shape, giving it a slightly pointed nose.

9 Insert the point of a knitting needle in the pompom where you want to place the eyes and squeeze a small blob of adhesive into each. Using the tweezers, place a black bead on each blob of adhesive.

10 Cut a tiny triangle of pink felt. Coat the back with adhesive and, using the tweezers, position to form a nose.

11 Cut two rectangles of cream felt, each about ⅝ x 1¼in (1.5 x 3cm). Shape one end of each into a point to form the outer ear.

12 Cut two inner ears from pink felt, making each slightly narrower and shorter than the cream outer ears. Coat the back of each with adhesive and fix in place.

13 Part the yarn on one side of the head using the blade of the scissors. Squeeze adhesive along the channel formed and push in the ear, pink side to front, and pinch the yarn over it to secure. Repeat on the other side for the other ear.

14 Cut a rectangle of felt that is about 1½ x ⅜in (4 x 1cm). Spread both sides with a thin layer of adhesive and dip into the reserved pompom trimmings to coat the tail. Insert and fix in place as for the ears.

15 Check the shape of the lamb, trimming if necessary to produce the desired effect.

Snowman

On cold winter days this jolly fellow will put a smile on your face. Enhance the frosty effect by using ice-white cotton yarn and leaving the pompoms slightly shaggy.

Materials

Medium and large pompom makers
About 50g of DK cotton or cotton-mix yarn
Oddment of green DK or 4-ply yarn
A brown chenille stick
2 x black 5–6mm beads
Scrap of red felt
All-purpose adhesive
Sharp scissors
Darning needle
Pair of 4mm knitting needles
Small round-nose pliers
Pointed tweezers
Pencil
Clothes pegs or paper clip

Method

1 Make one medium and one large pompom, leaving the ends used to tie them together long. Trim very lightly to create the frosty effect.

2 Knot the pompoms together securely, then thread the darning needle on each end of yarn individually and sew back and forth through both pompoms several times for extra security.

3 Using the pliers, twist one end of the chenille stick into a hand shape as shown in the photograph.

4 Poke the other end through the top of the larger pompom, then twist the other end into a hand shape. Part the yarn on the pompom and squeeze in adhesive to fix the arm in place. Allow the adhesive to dry.

5 Part the yarn on the head using the end of a pencil at the point where you want to place each eye, then squeeze a small blob of adhesive into each indentation. Using the tweezers, position the eyes.

6 Cut a small triangle from the red felt and roll to form a nose, secure with adhesive and hold in place with a peg or paper clip while it dries.

7 Add a little more adhesive to the base of the nose. Part the yarn with the pencil and push the nose firmly in, pinching the yarn over it to secure.

8 Using the green yarn, cast on five stitches and work in garter stitch for 12in (30cm). Cast off and sew in the yarn ends.

9 Tie the scarf round the neck of the snowman.

Tip

Small twigs may also be used as arms instead of the chenille stick.

Teddy

It's incredibly easy to make a teddy on a small scale using pompoms. Enhance the effect by choosing a textured mohair yarn.

Materials

Small and medium
    pompom makers
Brown, textured mohair or
    shaggy DK yarn
2 x small teddy bear eyes or
    5mm black beads
Scrap of black felt or EVA sheet
Short length of narrow ribbon
All-purpose adhesive
Sharp scissors
Darning needle
Pointed tweezers
Knitting needle or pencil

Method

1. Make one small and one medium pompom, leaving the ends of yarn used to tie them off long. Do not trim the pompoms at this stage.

2. Knot the pompoms securely together. Thread the lengths of yarn on the darning needle, one at a time, and sew back and forth through both pompoms for extra security.

3. Make four small pompoms and sew them firmly in place on the front and sides of the body to form the legs and arms.

4. Make two very small pompoms, but wind them using only about half the usual amount of yarn. Trim to size and sew in place on the top of the head to form ears.

5. Part the yarn using a knitting needle or pencil at the points where you want to place the eyes. Squeeze a small blob of adhesive in each.

6. Push the eyes firmly into position, then set aside and allow the adhesive to dry.

7. Cut a tiny circle from the felt or EVA sheet. Coat the back with adhesive and press into place for the nose.

8. Check the appearance of your teddy and trim carefully as necessary. You may need to trim the arms slightly to shape them.

9. Tie the ribbon round the teddy's neck.

Dog

Upright and alert with a shiny nose and bright button eyes, this little dog seems like the ideal pet. A length of broken bracelet makes a perfect choke chain.

Materials

Very small, small, medium
and large pompom makers
Cream wool DK yarn
Triangular toy nose
2 x 5–6mm black beads
Scrap of cream felt
All-purpose adhesive
Sharp scissors
Large darning needle
Pointed tweezers
Short length of chain
Clothes pegs
Pencil

Method

1   Make one large and one medium pompom. Trim well, leaving the ends of yarn used to tie them off long.

2   Knot the pompoms firmly together. Thread the ends of the yarn, one at a time, on the darning needle and run them back and forth through both pompoms several times to secure.

3   Make four small pompoms, leaving the ends used to tie them off long. Attach the pompoms to the base of the large pompom by sewing them in securely.

4   Make a very small pompom, using a little less yarn than usual so it is not too spherical. Attach to the head to form a nose. The angle at which you place this pompom will determine which way your dog's head faces.

5   Using sharp scissors, trim the dog carefully into a pleasing shape. Trim the nose so that it is fairly flat and wide. Do not throw away the trimmings as you will need them for the ears and tail.

6   Turn the dog upside-down and trim each of the four small pompoms to produce a flat base for the dog to sit on.

Tip

An old narrow leather watch strap also makes an effective collar.

7 Insert the point of a pencil into the pile of the head just above the nose, where you want to place the eyes. Squeeze a blob of adhesive into each indentation and, using the tweezers, carefully position the eyes. Allow the adhesive to dry.

8 Make an indentation where you want to place the nose. Squeeze in a blob of adhesive and insert the nose, pushing it in well.

9 Cut two rectangles of cream felt, each about ¾ x 1¼in (1.5 x 3cm). Curve the end of each rectangle to form an ear shape.

10 Cover one side of each ear with adhesive and dip into the pompom trimmings, pressing well so the ear is coated with fluff. Set aside to dry.

11 Cut a rectangle of felt as before and shape to make a tail. You can make this any size or length you like. Coat with pompom trimmings, as for the ears.

12 Using the blade of the scissors, part the head pompom at the side where you want to place the first ear. Squeeze in adhesive and insert the ear, pinching the pompom over the join to secure. Repeat with the other ear. Allow to dry, holding the ears in place with pegs if necessary.

13 Insert the tail between the two rear 'leg' pompoms, following the method used for the ears.

14 When the dog is completely dry, go over it with scissors to make sure you are happy with the shape.

15 Place a length of chain round the neck, closing it using the pliers.

Pot stand

This super-thick mat will protect your table from hot pots as well as look beautiful. If you want to hang up your mat when it's not in use, add a crocheted or ribbon loop.

Materials

Small pompom maker
Dark and light shades
    of DK yarn
4in (10cm) circular plastic
    canvas mat
Square of felt slightly
    larger than mat
All-purpose adhesive
Sharp scissors
Clothes pegs

Tip
Wool or wool-mix yarns make the best insulators for mats.

Method

1 Lay the plastic canvas on the felt and cut out a circle about ½in (1cm) larger all round for backing the mat.

2 Make enough pompoms in a dark shade of yarn to fit round the edge of the plastic canvas when butted closely against each other. For the mat shown, 12 pompoms were used.

3 Trim the pompoms into firm spheres, leaving the yarn ends used to tie them off long.

4 Thread the long ends of yarn of the first pompom on a large needle and sew through the adjacent holes on the edge of the plastic canvas, tying them firmly at the back to secure them. You may find this easier if you mark the rough position of each pompom on the canvas before you begin. Repeat until all the pompoms are attached.

5 Make a pompom in a dark shade of yarn and fasten to the centre of the canvas as before.

6 Make enough pompoms in light shades of yarn to fill in the gap between the centre and edge pompoms. For the example shown, seven pompoms were used. Tie in position.

7 Part each pompom where it joins the next and squeeze a line of adhesive in the gap. This will help to keep your mat together. Allow the adhesive to dry.

8 Turn the mat over and trim the tying threads closely using sharp scissors.

9 Cover one side of the felt circle with a thin layer of adhesive and press firmly to the mat, making sure that the circumference adheres to the pompoms. Peg in place at intervals and allow the adhesive to dry.

10 Using sharp scissors, trim the whole mat to flatten the pompoms slightly and provide a level base for your pot.

Heart

Show someone how much you care with this chunky red heart shot through with a golden Cupid's arrow.

Materials

Large pompom maker
50g of red 4-ply or DK yarn
Small square of yellow felt
Yellow chenille stick
All-purpose adhesive
Sharp scissors
Knitting needle or chopstick
Clothes peg or paper clip

Method

1 Make a large pompom, winding the yarn very closely to produce a dense final effect.

2 Using sharp scissors, trim the pompom into an oval shape, then trim the front and back to produce a flattened oval.

3 Carefully trim one end of the oval into a point, working on just a few strands at a time until you are happy with the effect.

4 Part the opposite end of the oval in the centre and trim the first few strands on each side fairly short. Trim the next few strands, leaving them slightly longer than the first layer. Repeat until the centre top of the heart is nicely indented.

5 Fold the chenille stick sides to the middle and twist to secure. Insert a knitting needle or chopstick in the loop on one end and wind round to produce a twisted effect. Repeat with the other side.

6 Cut a triangle from the felt, making each side about 1⁹⁄₁₆in (4cm) long. Coat one side of the triangle with adhesive and fold over one end of the twisted chenille stick. Hold in place with a clothes peg or paper clip until the adhesive dries.

7 Cut a 1⁹⁄₁₆in (4cm) square from yellow felt. Using sharp scissors, snip 1³⁄₁₆in (3cm) into the square at intervals to create a fringed effect. Coat the unfringed end of the square with adhesive and wrap round the other end of the twisted chenille stick, holding it in place with a peg or paper clip until the adhesive dries.

8 Run the blade of your scissors diagonally across the front of the heart, parting the strands to form a groove.

9 Squeeze a line of adhesive along the groove and lay the chenille arrow along it, pinching the yarn together to cover the twisted stick. Set aside to dry.

Wreath

A wreath can be an all-year-round decoration if you choose pompoms made from yarn that complements your home décor. It's also a great project for using up all those yarn oddments.

Materials

Plastic canvas
Very small, small and medium
　　pompom makers
Yarn oddments in toning shades
All-purpose adhesive
Felt for backing
Length of ribbon or silk cord
Plate and bowl for template
Sharp scissors
Clothes pegs

Method

1　Mark out a circle on the plastic canvas or cardboard by drawing around a plate (size used here was approx. 10in/60cm). Position a small bowl in the centre of the circle and draw an inner circle. Cut out the template.

2　Place the template on the felt backing, draw round and cut out. Set the backing felt aside.

3　Make enough medium-sized pompoms to fit round the edge of the template. Trim, leaving the long ends of yarn used to tie them to attach them to the canvas.

4　Attach the pompoms by threading through the holes in the plastic canvas and tying firmly on the reverse.

5　Repeat Steps 3 and 4 to line the inner edge of the template.

6　Make an assortment of small and finger or fork pompoms (see Techniques section, pages 46–47) in different shades and weights of yarn. Trim and cut off the long ends of yarn.

7　Using all-purpose adhesive, fill in any gaps between the medium pompoms with tiny pompoms.

8　Turn the wreath over and trim all the tied ends of yarn short.

9　Apply an even layer of adhesive to the felt circle and press firmly in place on the reverse of the plastic canvas. If necessary, hold in place with clothes pegs placed at regular intervals until the adhesive dries.

10 Thread the ribbon or cord on to a large darning needle and push through the top of the wreath from front to back. Repeat with the other end to make a hanging loop. Adjust, then knot and trim ends.

Elasticated doll

This new take on the ever-popular rag doll is soft, cuddly and fun to make. The arms and legs are threaded on elastic to add to the fun.

Materials

Large, medium and
    small pompom makers
100g each of red, blue and
    green DK yarn
Oddments of cream and
    brown yarn
Two black buttons or toy eyes
Scrap of red felt
All-purpose adhesive
Length of ribbon
2yd (2m) of round cord elastic
Sharp scissors
Small crochet hook
Pencil

Method

1 Using blue yarn, make one large and one medium pompom for the doll's body. Do not cut off the long ends used to tie them.

2 Make eight small red pompoms, six green pompoms and six blue pompoms. Trim and cut off the ends of yarn used to tie them.

3 Make a triple knot in the end of a length of round cord elastic. Part a small red pompom carefully to reveal the slight hole in the centre where it was tied. Wrap the elastic round the crochet hook and draw the elastic very carefully through the pompom.

4 Repeat the process, threading the elastic through a blue, a green and another red pompom, then thread the elastic though the medium blue pompom. Hold the pompoms between fingers and thumb as you thread the elastic through to keep the strands of yarn in place.

5 Thread the elastic through a red, a green, a blue and finally another red pompom. Draw it up and make another triple knot. This completes the upper body and arms; the knots in the elastic will be hidden inside of the pompoms.

6 Using a length of elastic at least 12in (30cm) long, make a leg in a similar way using six pompoms for each, but do not cut off the elastic. Make another leg to match then tie the elastic together at the top of the legs.

Tip

Adding long plaits
or a ponytail
instantly turns it
into a girl doll.

11 Wrap brown yarn round a paperback book at least 50 times. Tie in the centre and cut through the ends to make a bunch of shaggy 'hair'. Do not cut the ends used to tie the bunch of hair.

12 Sew the bunch of yarn firmly into the top of the head, using the yarn ends.

13 Using the point of a pencil, make indentations in the yarn where you want to place the eyes. Squeeze in a blob of adhesive and press the eyes into position.

14 Cut a mouth shape from the scrap of red felt and use adhesive to attach it to the face.

15 Using sharp scissors, trim the hair into a shaggy, mop and trim any untidy area of the doll. Shape the hands, making sure that the knots in the elastic are well hidden.

16 Beginning with the front of the doll, part the yarn where the medium and large body pompoms join. Squeeze adhesive along the channel made and pinch the yarn together. Allow to dry.

17 Repeat with the back of the pompom, then do the same where the legs join the large pompom and the neck joins the medium one. It is best to do this one section at a time. Prop the doll up and allow the adhesive to dry.

18 Work over the whole doll with your scissors, flattening the outer curve on each of the pompoms and blending the joins between them. This stage takes quite a long time but it's important for the look of the finished doll.

19 Tie a length of ribbon round the doll's neck.

7 Take the large pompom and part the yarn to reveal the hole in the centre. Carefully draw both lengths of leg elastic through the centre of the pompom. Tie the elastic together at the top of the pompom using a double knot. This completes the lower body and legs.

8 Using the yarn ends left after tying the large and medium pompoms, sew them securely together to make the body. Take care to run the yarn round the elastic to make the join secure.

9 Make the head by winding a large pompom using cream yarn for one half and brown yarn for the other. Trim, leaving the ends used to tie the pompom long.

10 Using the yarn ends, join the head to the centre of the arm section, running the stitches round the elastic for security.

Planets mobile

Recreate the planets in the solar system with this funky mobile. Pluto is included in this model, but if you are a purist you might like to leave it out.

Materials

Oddments of yarn in browns, blues and oranges
Very small, small, medium and large pompom makers
Length of tree branch, dowelling or bamboo cane
Reel of nylon fishing line
Short length of flexible wire
Length of organza ribbon
Cup hook
Small piece of cardboard
'Superglue' adhesive
Sharp scissors

Planet	Size	Yarn
Sun	large	yellow
Mercury	small	brown
Venus	medium	red-brown
Earth	medium	blue and white
Mars	small	orange
Jupiter	large	beige
Saturn	medium	light brown
Uranus	medium	sky blue
Neptune	medium	mid-blue
Pluto	small	light brown

Method

1 Wind the pompoms as indicated, referring to the chart below for guidance. For Earth, wind mostly in blue adding irregular clumps of white at intervals.

2 Cut a circle of card slightly larger all round than 'Jupiter'. Cut a smaller hole in the centre. Wrap the card using beige yarn and secure the ends using a little adhesive. Push the circle over the 'Jupiter' pompom, easing the strands of yarn round the middle of the pompom and supported by the yarn strands.

3 Cut the length of wood in two, making one section slightly longer than the other. The example shown overleaf used a piece about 18in (46cm) long and a piece about 16in (41cm) long.

4 Using the wire, bind the two pieces of wood together in the shape of a cross. Do not worry too much about the effect, as it will be covered with ribbon.

5 Screw a cup hook into the top of the cross shape. Suspend the frame of the mobile from a doorway for ease of working as you assemble the components.

6 Cut a length of fishing line and thread it on the darning needle. Sew the line through the sun pompom, taking it over the yarn tie. Bring it back up again then knot the fishing line at the top of the pompom.

7 Decide how far you want the sun to hang down and tie a loop in the end. Push the sun to the centre of the mobile.

8 Position the remainder of the planets on the crossbars in the same way; the hanging stage may take a long time, as you should ensure that the crossbars balance. You should also be prepared for interference from any astrophysicists in the family!

9 Working from above, carefully dot a tiny amount of superglue on the top of each loop of fishing line to hold it in place.

10 Cover the wire at the centre of the crossbar with ribbon and give the planets a final trim.

Materials and equipment

Safety first
Pompoms are not suitable for babies, as they may pull out the short strands of yarn. However, mobiles that are hung safely out of reach will amuse them for hours. For young children, avoid beads or small parts that might be pulled off and use felt features instead.

Materials
Other than the key ingredient, which is of course yarn, you'll need just a few more materials to complete the projects in this book:

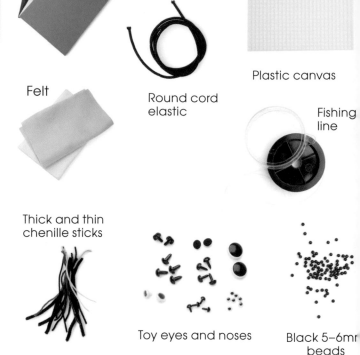

EVA sheet

Felt

Round cord elastic

Plastic canvas

Fishing line

Basic equipment
Pompom toys are wonderfully simple and therefore don't require a great deal of equipment. There are just a few basic items that you'll need to hand, which are as follows:

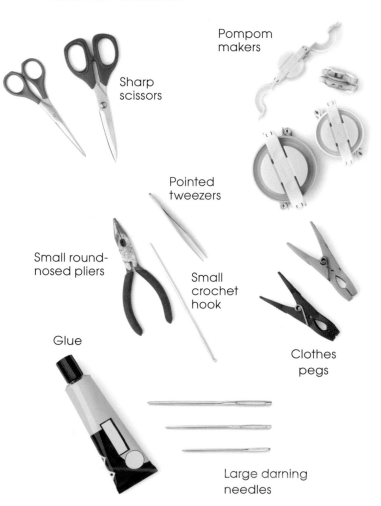

Sharp scissors

Pompom makers

Pointed tweezers

Small round-nosed pliers

Small crochet hook

Clothes pegs

Glue

Large darning needles

Thick and thin chenille sticks

Toy eyes and noses

Black 5–6mm beads

Choosing yarn
Pompoms may be made using many different types of yarn. Small pompoms look better made from 4-ply yarn, while very small or 'fork' pompoms are effective in 2-ply, fine mohair or lace-weight yarn. Double knitting yarn is a good all-rounder for medium and large pompoms, while for very large pompoms Aran-weight or even chunky yarn may also be used.

Experiment with different types, weights and textures of yarn to produce different effects – you can always make a funky garland using all your practice pompoms!

Techniques

Making pompoms

Pompoms may be made by the traditional method of using circles of card, but this is really time-consuming. A faster, fun option is to use special plastic pompom makers. Sets of these ingenious tools are widely available from craft or haberdashery departments or online. The type used for this book is sold in sets containing either a very small (1⅛in (30mm)) and a small (1⅝in (40mm)) pompom maker or a medium (2⅜in (60mm)) and a large (3⅛in (80mm)) pompom maker.

1 For best results, wind the yarn smoothly and evenly over the pompom maker, taking care to cover the outer edges. For a firm pompom, be sure to fill up each side of the pompom maker completely.

2 Cut the yarn strands a few at a time using sharp scissors, taking care not to dislodge the pompom maker.

3 To fasten off, tightly wrap the yarn once around the entire pompom maker then wrap the yarn again and tie using a double knot. If you think the yarn you have used is likely to break, tie the pompoms off using a toning colour of strong cotton thread or fine cotton yarn.

4 Open up the pompom maker and remove your pompom.

5 Fluff up the pompom and trim to shape.

Trimming

Depending on the effect you wish to achieve, trimming can be an important part of making pompoms. For a shaggy pompom, you may not want to trim at all. Pompoms can be shaped by carefully trimming them with sharp scissors – I use a pair of hairdressing scissors. It is possible to change the shape dramatically by trimming. For example, a shape that looks like five spheres tied together can be transformed into a realistic dog by careful trimming. Start small and trim tiny areas at a time, examining your work constantly. You will see your creation taking shape before your eyes.

Features

The right choice of eyes and nose can make a big difference to the appeal of a pompom toy. Small black beads can be used for the eyes of many animals, and plain black buttons also produce a good effect. Special animal eyes and noses are also available; these usually have a long shank that can be coated with adhesive and pushed into the pompom. Googly, self-adhesive eyes can be fun on certain animals or creatures. Haberdashery sections of department stores usually have a good selection and should provide plenty of inspiration.

Whiskers can be made using short lengths of nylon fishing line. Noses and beaks can be created using small pieces of felt that are cut to the correct shape. If you make a mistake or dislike the effect you have produced, ease them off before the adhesive dries and try again.

The legs of pompom creatures can be very easily made using chenille sticks (these used to be called pipe cleaners). For a thicker leg, twist two chenille sticks together. The sticks can also be wrapped with yarn to make them sturdier. If you do this, be sure to fasten off the ends using all-purpose adhesive.

A really attractive finish can be achieved by wrapping the legs with wool roving (unspun wool that is sold for felting), then securing the ends with adhesive.

Tiny pompoms

Really small pompoms are most successful when made using fine yarn such as 2- or 3-ply. Laceweight or fine mohair is ideal. There are three ways to make tiny pompoms. One way is to make them on a small pompom maker and then trim them down to the size you require, but this wastes quite a lot of yarn. The other methods are using your fingers or an ordinary dinner fork with four tines; the latter option is the one to go for if you're after really tiny pompoms. For both finger and fork pompoms, it is best to tie them off using strong cotton thread in a toning shade.

Fork pompoms

For really tiny pompoms, use an ordinary dinner fork with four tines.

1   Wind the yarn round, halfway up the tines, then push a threaded needle into the gap between the second and third tines and the bowl of the fork.

2   Bring the needle up to the front of the fork, take it down round the yarn and tie off tightly.

3   Slip the tied yarn carefully off the fork and cut the doubled strands.

4   Fluff out the pompom and trim to shape.

Finger pompoms

1. Wind the yarn round your fingers between 30 and 50 times, depending on the weight of yarn.

2. Take a darning needle threaded with strong cotton and insert it in the gap between your fingers, then bring it up again between your fingertips.

3. Tie as tightly as possible, enlisting help if necessary, as this can be fiddly.

4. Ease the tied loops of yarn from your fingers, then cut through the loops on either side of the tie.

5. Fluff out the pompom and trim to shape.

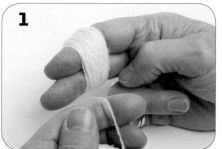

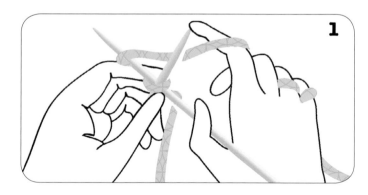
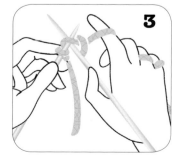

Knitting techniques

Casting on

1. Form a slip knot on the left needle. Insert the right needle into the loop and wrap yarn around it as shown.

2. Pull the yarn through the first loop to create a new one.

3. Slide it onto the left-hand needle. There are now two stitches on the left needle. Continue in this way until you have the required number of stitches.

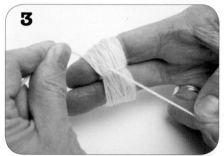

Knit stitch / Garter stitch

1 Hold the needle with the cast-on stitches in your left hand. Place the tip of the empty right needle into the first stitch and wrap the yarn around as for casting on.

2 Pull the yarn through to create a new loop.

3 Slip the newly made stitch onto the right needle.

Note: For garter stitch, knit every stitch.

Casting off

1 Knit two stitches onto the right needle, then slip the first stitch over the second stitch and let it drop off the needle (one stitch remains).

2 Knit another stitch so you have two stitches on the right needle again. Repeat the process until there is only one stitch on the left needle. Break the yarn and thread it through the remaining stitch to fasten off.

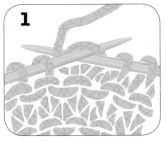

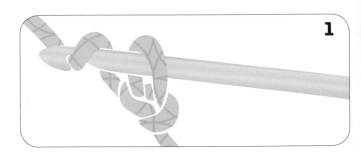

Crochet techniques
Chain stitch (ch)

1 With the hook in your right hand and the yarn resting over the middle finger of your left hand, pull the yarn taut. Take the hook under, then over the yarn.

2 Pull the hook and yarn through the loop while holding the slip knot steady. Repeat to form a foundation row of chain stitch (ch).

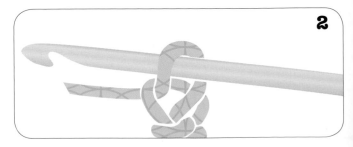